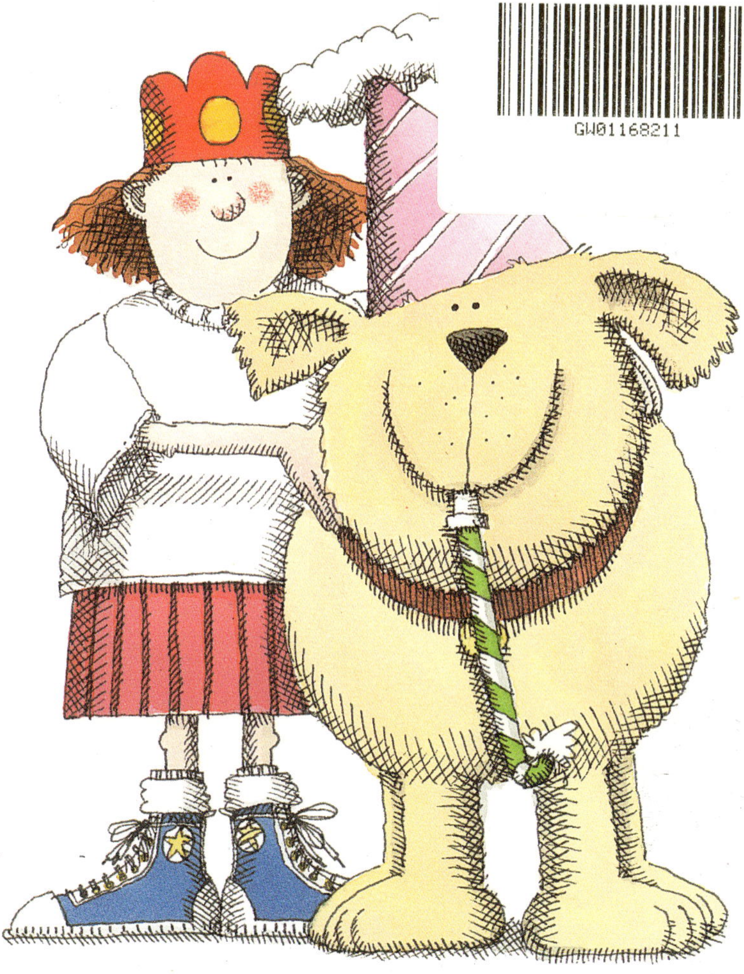

My dog had a party.

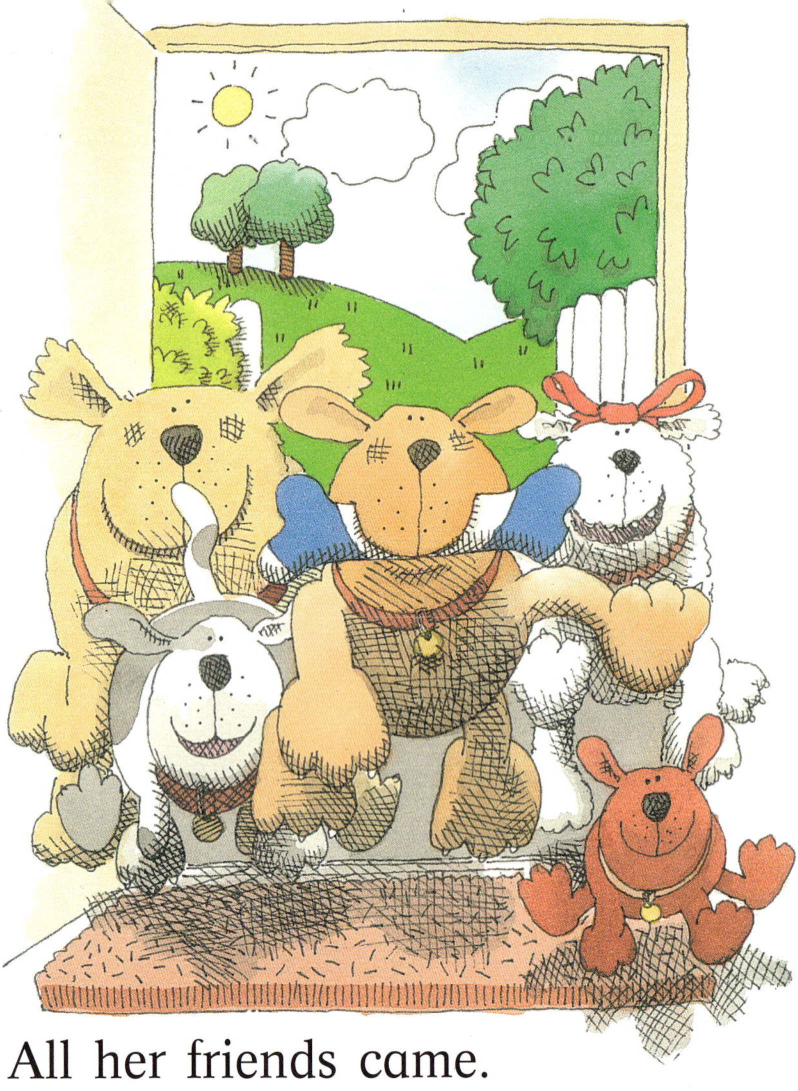

All her friends came.

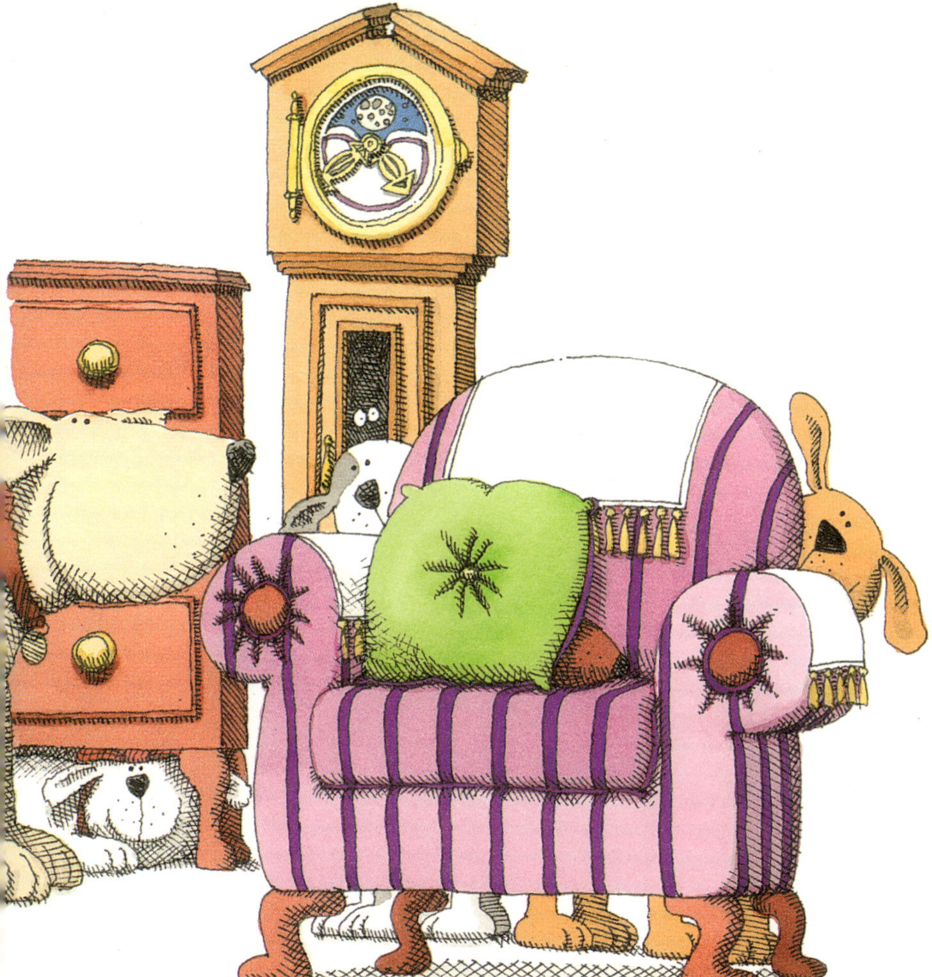

They played hide and seek.

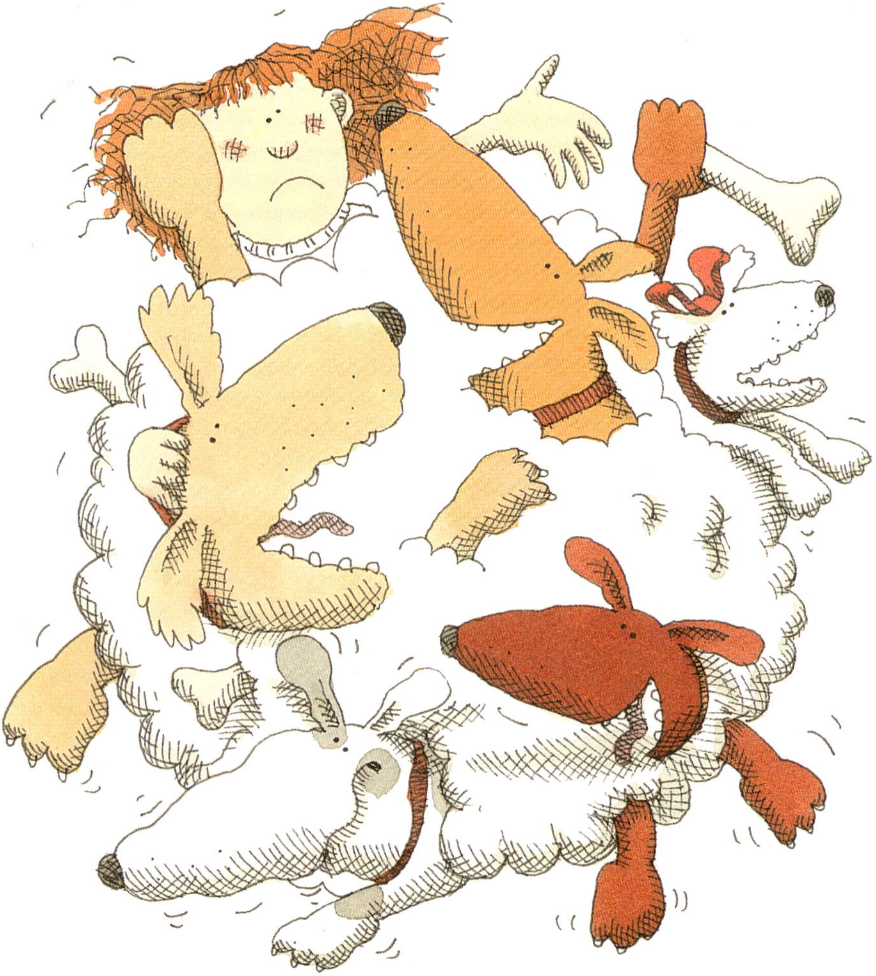

They had a fight.

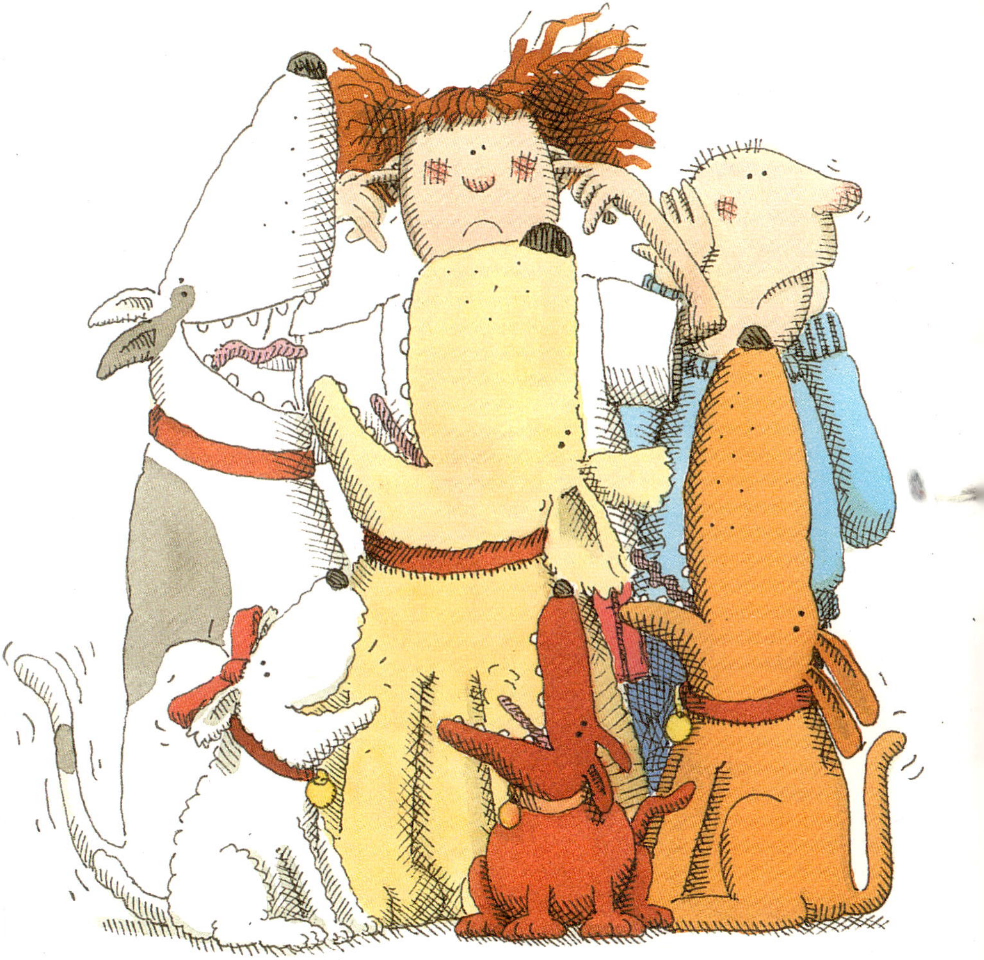

They sang us a song.

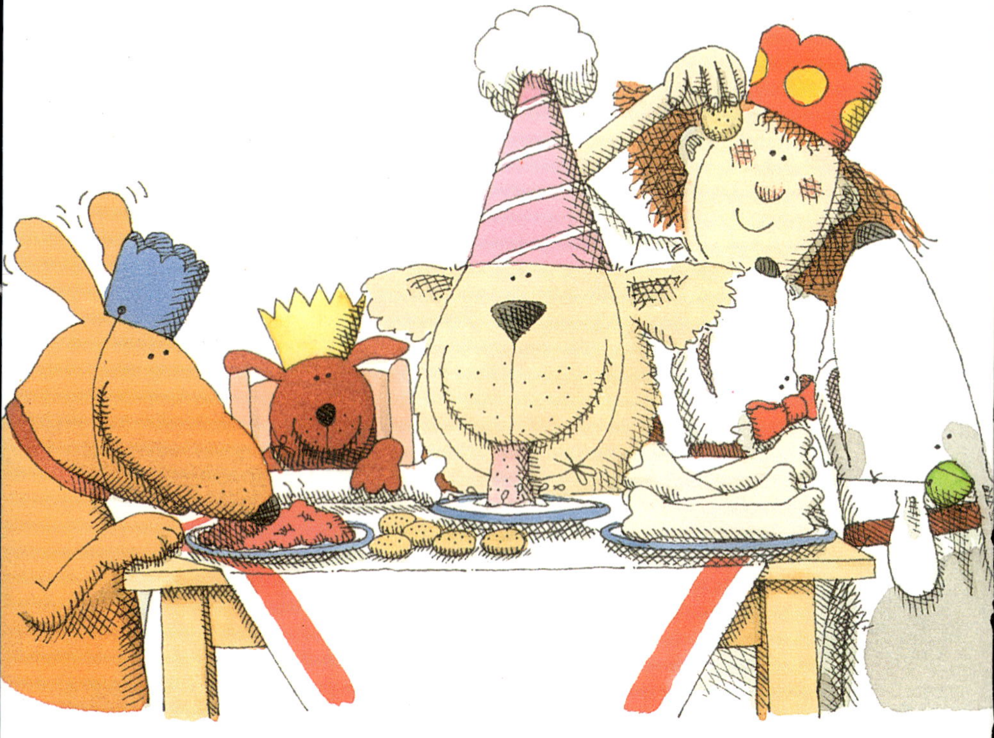

Then they had tea.

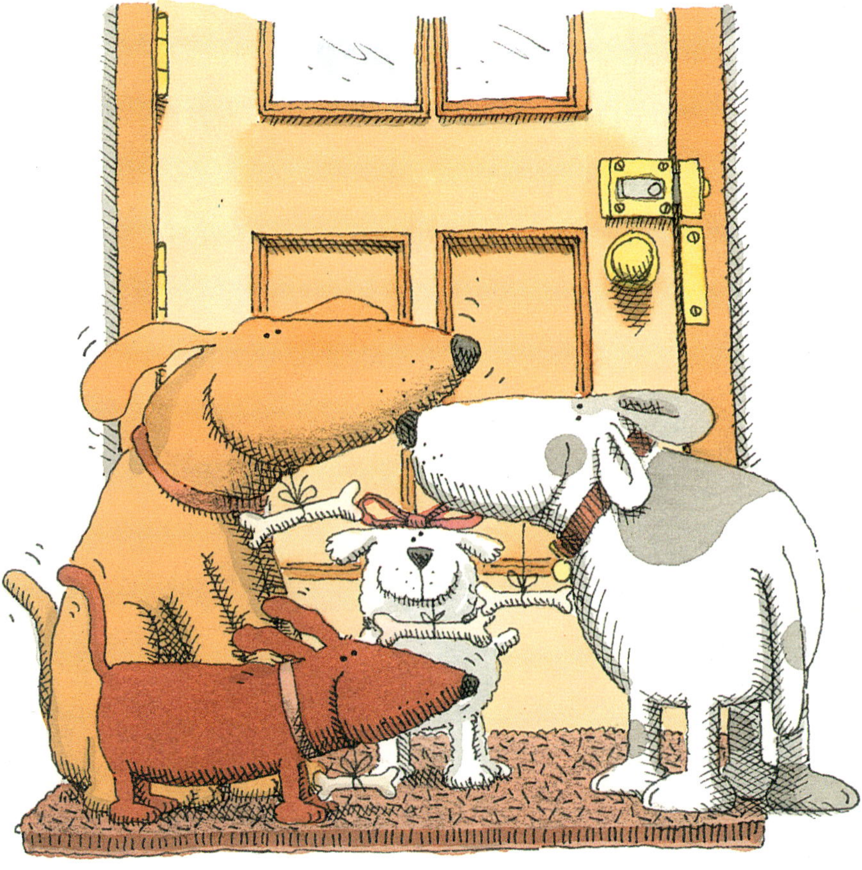

And when they went home,

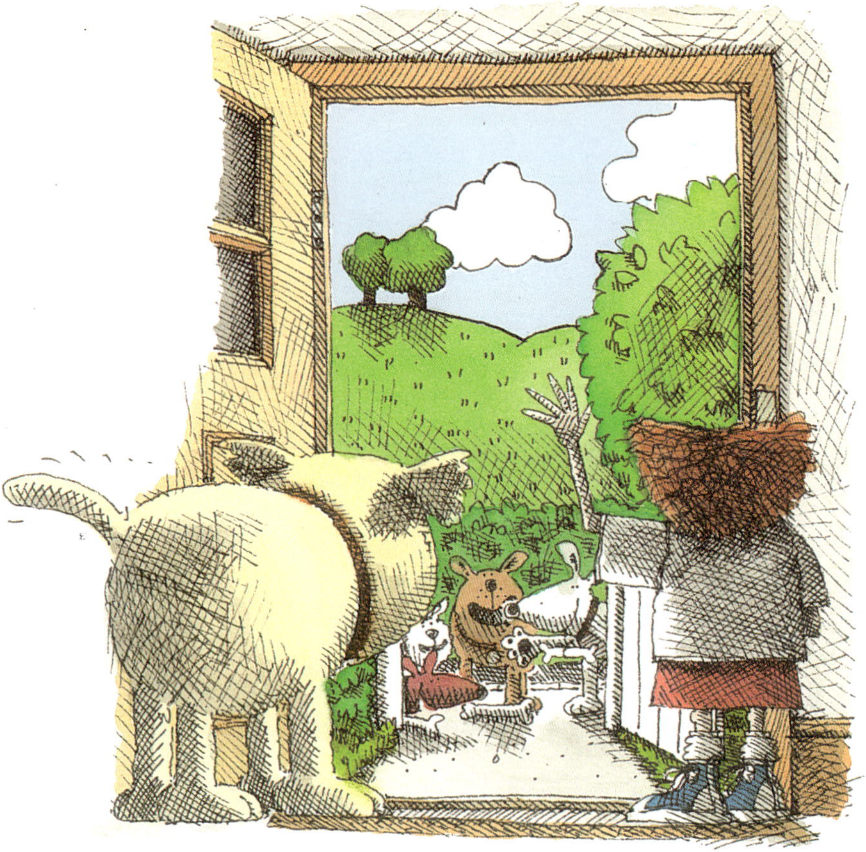

they all said, "Thank you!"